# The Franchise
# RULES

## Michael Martuza

# Copyright

The Franchise RULES

© 2014, Michael Martuza

# Table of Contents

# Terminology

A few basic franchise definitions are below. For a more in-depth list, type *franchise terminology* into any browser.

**Discovery Day (a.k.a. D-Day or Meet the Team Day):** Discovery Day is an event that is conducted by most franchise companies for their best candidates. The candidate visits the franchise company's headquarters where he/she is able to meet the team of people he/she will be working with as a franchise owner.

**Franchise Disclosure Document (a.k.a. FDD):** A Franchise Disclosure Document is the franchising equivalent of a stock or mutual fund prospectus. The Federal Trade Commission (FTC) regulates the content and layout of this document. The franchise company must update the FDD at least once per year and provide you a current copy in the early stages of your investigation.

**Franchise Attorney:** An attorney who specializes in the writing and/or reviewing of FDDs.

**Franchise Broker:** An individual who acts as an intermediary between the franchise company and an interested franchise buyer. The potential franchise buyer incurs no cost for these services. The franchise company pays the broker a commission.

**Franchisee:** An owner of a franchise location.

**Franchisor:** The franchise company.

**Wildebeest:** A member of the antelope family and one of the favorite snack foods of African crocodiles.

# Introduction

As a first business I have found that a franchise is by far the best option for most people. When looking for your first business, you will have either general business expertise or functional expertise. Very few first-time business owners have both. The owner of an independent (non-franchised) business needs to make excellent business and functional decisions from Day 1. When a problem arises in a non-franchised business, it's hard for the owner to seek guidance from his/her peers because they will probably be the competition. This leaves the owner to make a "best guess" and hope for a good result. One reason so many new, non-franchised businesses fail in the first few years is that the owner's "best guess" is not only wrong, but also fatal.

Franchised businesses avoid the need for the owner to "know everything" from Day 1. If you have issues or problems, then not only is the franchise company there to help you, but so are the other franchise owners; you're part of the team, not the competition. Think about it as being "on your own, but never alone." In addition, the owner's responsibility is more manageable as the franchise company will usually tend to the backend systems while asking the owner to focus on the customer/client side (i.e., growing the business). Continual development and evolution of systems (e.g., technical, marketing, operations, etc.) and the business expertise are part of why you're considering joining a franchise rather than doing it yourself.

In the past decade I've spoken with many people who say they no longer want to work for someone else. They're tired of the uncertainty that goes along with corporate jobs and creating financial rewards for others. These are people who want to be in control of their future.

Contrary to the thinking of some, being a successful franchise owner requires a lot more than just plopping down a pile of money and waiting for the profits to roll in. I know many franchise owners; some are extremely successful while others struggle. In most cases the difference between the two groups is not the skill or dedication of the owner, but his/her 'fit' with the franchise system.

During my years as both an owner and broker of franchised businesses, I'm frequently asked how to find a great 'fitting' franchise. Without realizing it I developed rules that help guide my clients to find that great 'fit.' Does following these rules guarantee success? Of course not, but doing so will greatly increase the probability.

I have tried to make this book as easy to read as possible with what I believe are rules that should always be followed. The examples I use throughout this book are real, although for obvious reasons I've omitted the names of the people and companies.

Thanks for buying and reading this book.

Mike

Mike@TheFranchiseRULES.com

# Chapter 1: Before You Begin

## *Read This Part First!*

(After the Introduction, of course. Also, don't forget the footnotes).

# Rule 1: Don't Do Anything Stupid!

I know that the phrasing of this rule may seem a bit harsh, but periodically we all need to be reminded that sometimes we do things on impulse that we later regret.

Everyone has, at one time or another, been caught up in an emotional wave and done something he/she later regrets before the rational thought process catches up. Making big money decisions when your logical side is being beaten into submission by your emotional side is a favorite tactic of most businesses that rely upon immediate and/or one-time sales. Have you bought, or know someone else who has bought, a time-share vacation condo and come to regret it soon thereafter? In a 2- or 3-hour session, the condo salesperson will continually emphasize the amenities, the flexibility, the cost savings, and the family time you will gain over the years. The pitch sounds so convincing that, by the end of the session, even the most frugal, skeptical person has a harder time saying "No."

How do you investigate franchise opportunities without getting caught up in a wave of emotion and make your decisions based upon logic? Seek the help and guidance of people who understand the nuances of the franchise industry. The rules that follow will help you find the right people; those that will help you evaluate franchises logically and rationally, and find one that is a great 'fit.'

# Rule 2: The Road Less Taken.

Determining if business ownership is the right choice may seem like an easy task, but most of the decisions we make are influenced by the same decisions we've made in the past. For example, when I left college many years ago I had to decide whether to work for myself or someone else. At that time, working for someone else best 'fit' my short-term goals of an assured income and benefits.[1] When it came time to move to the next opportunity, the decision to work for someone else or myself was influenced by my previous choice. For the first 15 years of my career, every decision became more and more subconsciously influenced by my past choices. I didn't think about whether my goals had changed and if the best path forward was still the same.

**Two Paths – One Goal**

---

[1] As I was young, single, and poor I was not thinking much about long-term goals.

Selecting a path forward, be it business ownership or job, is secondary to understanding what you want to accomplish in your life (i.e. what is your destination?). The Roman philosopher Seneca said, "If one does not know to which port one is sailing, no wind is favorable." Everyone has his/her own idea of success (both short- and long-term); if you don't know what you're trying to accomplish prior to starting your journey, it's going to be very hard to reach your destination.

If you're thinking about buying a franchise (or getting another job), take the time to re-evaluate your goals before you begin. Have they changed since the last time you really looked at them? Once you understand more about your destination (some future combination of financial and lifestyle elements), all you're doing is determining which path is most likely to get you there from your starting point.

# Rule 3: When I Grow Up I Want To Be A...

Many people in the career transition groups that I work with have said, "I still don't know what I want to be when I grow up." This is interesting because they're in their 50's or 60's and still looking for a career that makes them happy.

Work doesn't have to make you miserable, although the thought of actually enjoying yourself while making money seems to be a concept that many have a hard time comprehending.

When you first meet someone, it is inevitable that within the first few minutes you will be asked, "What do you do?" The answer to this question is very important since what you do (or your title) may define who you are and determine your position within the social hierarchy. For most, your job (or title) is as important to your status as the size of the antlers is to a moose.

Awhile back I was fortunate enough to connect with a mentor who helped me realize that the "When I grow up..." question should not take a job or title perspective, but should be looked at as a combination of an end goal and my level of happiness while achieving that goal. Like many others, I have a long-term goal of "financial security," but I want to enjoy myself as I achieve it.

Remaining on the road that provides the best opportunity to achieve our goals may, at times, be difficult. Periodically we are required to make career or lifestyle choices where the most attractive option in the short-term could put us on a road leading far away from our desired long-term destination.

For example, many years ago when I was a corporate executive, I was offered a position at a different company for twice my salary. I enjoyed my then current position – it paid well, intellectually challenged me, and had reasonable hours. Although the prospect of doubling my salary was a powerful lure, after much consideration, I declined the offer; my friends and colleagues thought that I was nuts. I knew that if I had accepted the offer, once the novelty of the huge salary increase wore off, I would have been miserable because the job wouldn't have challenged me intellectually or creatively, and I would have been required to work long hours leaving me with no personal life. In essence, it came down to ignoring the shiny object placed in front of me and focusing on my end goal of balancing work satisfaction, financial reward and enjoyment of life.

# Rule 4: End of the Road?

After a recent franchise workshop, several members of the audience stayed to talk further. One person made the following statement: "I can't find a job, which is what my wife and I really want, so I think that I'll have to buy a franchise instead." My response caught him by surprise. I told him, "Buying a business should not result solely from running out of all other options."

There's no middle ground when it comes to owning any business, including a franchise. Successful business owners are driven by internal factors that lead them to believe they will be happier, more fulfilled, and more successful owning a business than working for someone else. This driving force is independent of the ability to find a job; they don't really want a job.

There is always an increased level of anxiety associated with change (think about the times you have switched jobs or companies). Even very successful people are nervous in new situations. But, they also have a strong belief that they will succeed based upon their past successes. Why would you agree to move to a new situation if you expected to fail?

If you start with the mentality that owning a business is the last option, then your chances of succeeding are very small, much like if you accepted a job for which you were unqualified just because it was offered to you.

# Rule 5: Brain Clutter.

When selecting a franchise, one of the biggest hurdles to overcome is a potential bias toward the product or service that the business offers. It's important to keep an open mind because the best 'fitting' franchise for you may be in an industry in which you have misconceptions or never considered.

I'm not referring to a bias that is based upon legal, moral, or ethical principles. I'm referring to people who will go through a list of franchises and eliminate those based upon nothing other than what the business does.

I was once taught that when I start a sentence with "I know…" it signaled that I was no longer open to learning any more about that subject; it's like I slammed the door on my brain, cutting off any and all contradictory information. I come across this "I know…" mentality frequently when speaking about franchises. Phrases like "I know franchising is not for me because…" or "I know that a franchise in that industry would not be a good 'fit' for me because…" are usually based on nothing more than misconceptions. This doesn't mean that the conclusion is incorrect, but when the methodology is wrong, the likelihood of the conclusion being wrong increases.

Let's use a real example. One of the franchises I work with has the following attributes:

1. The cost to get the business open is about $100K.

2. Neither the owner nor the employees need to work nights, holidays, or weekends.

3. The "sales" effort is limited to providing quotes to those who call after receiving a direct mail coupon (i.e. the "sales" effort is low).

4. Greater than 50% of owners have advanced degrees (MBA, PhD, etc.).

5. Sales for the top third of franchise owners average about $1.5M.

6. Profit margin for owners in the top third is around 20%.

Solely based on these attributes, I've had many clients interested in learning more about this concept. Most had their interest fade when they found out that this is a residential cleaning (maid) franchise. Did your interest in the business change when you found out what it was? If so, you may have a lot of brain clutter that is blocking new ideas, ones that may be crucial for you to find great 'fitting' opportunities. Should I send one of the maids over to clean out the clutter for you?

During workshops I'm often asked if I will provide a list of the franchise companies with whom I work. I understand that a person may feel that he/she is missing out on something if every option is not known upfront. I'll explain to him/her that I never provide a list because I don't want anyone to eliminate concepts based on preconceived notions before we have a discussion. I'd rather learn about my client's goals, skills, and budget, and then eliminate concepts based upon 'fit' and ability to succeed, rather than the industry.

# Rule 6: We Won!  They Lost...

Many have trouble taking responsibility for anything that goes wrong in their life (business and/or personal). On the other hand, it's really easy for them to take all of the credit when something good happens.  Blaming others is just easier, whether it's avoiding unpleasant feedback from another person (e.g., boss or spouse) or avoiding a self-inflicted hit to the ego.  The act of blaming others is learned as a child when caught doing something wrong and trying to avoid punishment.  Blaming others continues into the job world where, in the matrix structure of many companies, it's easy to shift blame as job definitions and responsibilities can be vague.  We even disassociate ourselves from failure in the sports teams we support.  When a team that you and your friends support wins, listen for the phrase "we won".  But if your team loses listen how the same people will distance themselves by changing the phrase to "they lost."

When you own a business, assigning blame to others doesn't work.  The sooner you accept the notion that EVERYTHING is your fault, the more likely you will be successful.  I've seen franchise owners blame the systems, the franchise company's headquarters people, the economy, the geographic region, and a host of other excuses to explain their lack of success, except themselves.

The only way to have control over the outcomes in your life is to accept responsibility for everything (positive and negative) that happens to you. By taking responsibility, you take control. Taking control allows you to learn from mistakes and fix them so they don't happen again. If you blame others, you've lost control and are inviting the same problems to happen over and over.

# Rule 7: Are You A Wildebeest?

Without the support of your spouse (or significant other) it makes no sense to consider business ownership. You're wasting your time unless you're considering a divorce (or separation).

A phenomenon that I deal with frequently is "spousal ambush." Often one person will begin the process of looking for a franchise, while the partner keeps his/her distance, neither encouraging nor discouraging the activities. The passive partner doesn't wish to participate in any part of the search process (e.g., discussions with a franchise broker, informational literature or videos, discussions with the franchise company or franchise owners, etc.), but will tell the active partner to do all of the work and come back when there is only one concept remaining. After 2 or 3 months of work by the active partner, what do you think happens?

This scenario ends the same almost 100% of the time. Imagine the TV nature shows that highlight the animals of the Serengeti. The wildebeest migration that occurs every year takes these animals across a river inhabited by hungry crocodiles that are lying in wait. As the wildebeest approaches its destination (the opposite river bank), the croc catches a leg in its jaws and after a struggle drags the wildebeest under.

"Spousal ambush" works the same way. You'll put in all of the hours and obtain all of the information you need to find a great 'fitting' franchise. Then, only after all the work has been completed and you're thinking that you're almost to your short-term destination (business ownership), your spouse tells you in no uncertain terms that you're not buying a business, but rather you're getting a job that provides benefits and a steady paycheck.  No matter how much resistance you put up, the spouse (croc) is going to win.

With that in mind it's VERY important to get your partner on board early!  He/she does not have to be jumping up and down with excitement over the prospect of owning a business, but he/she does have to be supportive and willing to participate in the process.  If your partner wants you to get a job and earn a steady paycheck, that's probably where you'll end up.  It's better to know this up front so you don't waste months of valuable job search time.

Having the support of your spouse will matter even beyond the business versus job debate.  I've found that the likelihood of finding a great 'fitting' franchise increases the more the spouse is involved.  Why is this?  Because identifying and evaluating our own strengths and weaknesses is a very difficult task.  Having someone who knows you better than anyone else, who can provide an outside perspective, will be invaluable to your long-term success.  Your spouse can provide a logical assessment of your strengths and weaknesses (a BIG reality check for some), helping you stay away from an emotional decision that may result in buying a business that is a poor 'fit.'

# Rule 8: Yesterday Is Paid For, But Tomorrow Isn't Free.

The cost of buying and opening a franchise is not your only financial consideration when thinking about owning a business. To keep things simple, we're only going to focus on the costs for those franchises that require your full time involvement. [2]

The costs involved in buying and opening a franchise include:

1. Franchise Fee: A fixed cost per location or territory (the same for everyone). With this fee you're buying the experience, systems, training, expertise, and, in the case of a consumer offering, the brand name.

2. All other costs to get the business open: This encompasses a wide range of items that may include insurance, computers, location build out, equipment, initial supplies, and more. All required items are listed in the Franchise Disclosure Document (FDD) with an estimated cost. [3]

---

[2] There are semi-absentee franchises that are designed so that those who have a job and want to keep it can do so while building a business. With a semi-absentee business you don't, in most cases, have to worry as much about living expenses since you are working.

[3] The franchise will provide a cost range (low and high) for each item.

3. Working Capital: The amount of money that you will spend in the business over the first several months. It's important to note that there is NO correlation between the number of months of working capital indicated in the FDD and the first breakeven month for the average franchise owner. A good rule of thumb is to at least double the franchise company's estimate.

Beyond buying, opening, and operating the business, you will need money to live, hopefully at your accustomed lifestyle. Although situations are different for everyone, assume that you will not be able to take any money out of the business (whether you're profitable or not) for at least the first year. Therefore, you should have enough available savings (or a working spouse) to pay the bills while the business grows. Note that the time frame can be even longer when you're opening a business that requires a storefront location (e.g., retail, food, auto). You may still be able to take money out after the business has been open a year, but it may take you a significant amount of time to find and build out a location. Thus, when you're planning on the amount of money you need to live, remember to add the additional time required to get a storefront business open.

# Rule 9: Boo!

Fear. Nerves. Anxiety. Cold feet. No matter what you want to call it, you're going to feel it as you think about buying a franchise. If you're not scared at some point in the process, you're in a very, very small minority. You've probably experienced similar feelings before other big events in your life, such as right before you got married, when you found out your first child was on the way, or even when you've changed jobs.

Right before and/or very soon after writing the check to the franchise company, a moment of panic will hit you. You will likely think, "What am I doing?" or "Is this really the right thing?" There are a couple of reasons this occurs.

1. Most people are used to receiving money (a paycheck) and the thought of spending and/or borrowing money without an assurance of an income is very unsettling.

2. Working for someone else is a known situation. You may not like it, but you have a good idea what to expect on a daily basis. If this is your first look into business ownership, the uncertainty of what's next can be a very powerful deterrent to those who crave structure and certainty.

Almost everyone I've ever worked with has experienced these feelings. I've helped many clients work through them to become very successful business owners. The key to dealing with this fear (both in yourself and your significant other) is to prepare yourself; know that it will occur and that you need to remain focused on the logical reasons you're buying a business.

# Rule 10: Only Leaves Grow On Trees.

Determine how you're going to pay for your franchise and begin working on the process/details as soon as possible. If you're planning on using anything other than your own liquid assets (e.g., cash, stocks, etc.), it's likely that this process will take almost as long as the franchise search. You don't want to be in a situation where you have a franchise selected and then realize that the financial part may take another 4 to 8 weeks; that will really kill your enthusiasm.

Here are some sources for financing your business. Get started early if you're thinking about using them.

- Bank Loan (SBA or Non-SBA)
- Home Equity or Second Mortgage
- IRA Rollover (a.k.a. Self-Directed IRA)
- An Investor (e.g., friend, relative, etc.)
- Business Partner (see **Rule 36: Business Partners**)

By going through the financing process early, you can determine which option is best. Starting your financial investigation isn't a commitment to borrow money or buy a franchise.

## The Government... A Gift Horse?

Somehow, somewhere, a number of people started to believe that grant money is available from the government (Federal, State, or Local) to help buy a business. I hate to be a bucket of cold water, but I think this is an urban legend. I don't know of anyone who has ever received a grant from the government, nor do I know of anyone who knows anyone who has (that's a bit confusing isn't it). The point is: don't get all excited about opening a business if you're counting on any government money.

By the way, if you, or anyone that you know personally, is ever successful obtaining grant money, please send me an e-mail and let me know the details, as I'm sure others would be interested.

# Chapter 2: General Franchise Rules

They Didn't Teach These Rules In School.

# Rule 11: Just Because It's a Franchise...

Just because it's a franchise doesn't mean that it's a good business opportunity! There are about 2800 franchises in the U.S., of which about 20% are great, 60% are good, and 20% make you want to hold your nose.

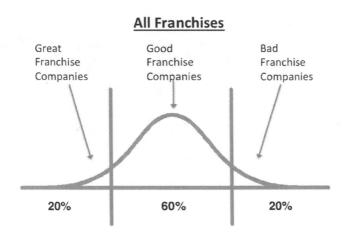

**All Franchises**

| Great Franchise Companies | Good Franchise Companies | Bad Franchise Companies |
|---|---|---|
| 20% | 60% | 20% |

What differentiates the great, the good, and the bad? Let's look at a few areas:

1. Franchise company/Franchise owner relationship:  Is it amicable and open? [4]

2. Quality of the franchise company's corporate staff: Are they experienced, understanding, responsive, and helpful?  Do they know their stuff?

---

[4] You will learn much more about this relationship during your due diligence calls with existing franchise owners.

3. Quality of the initial training and ongoing support: Is training comprehensive? Because initial training is usually overwhelming (think fire hose), are the support people responsive and helpful (even on the most basic questions) in your early months and years as an owner?

4. How/when does the franchise company make money: Do they have a "rising tide raises all boats" mentality? This means that they make their money from your royalties as you become successful, not from the upfront franchise fees. In other words, if you're successful, the franchise company is successful! On the opposite side are franchise companies with the mentality of "everyone into the deep end for a game of sink or swim." Many of the franchise companies with this mentality make their money from the franchise fees and don't put much emphasis on helping the franchise owners become successful.

5. Direction of the market/industry: Even the best of franchises will have a hard time if they are not keeping up with a changing market/industry.

6. Would the vast majority of current franchise owners buy the business again if they knew then what they know now?

Even some of the BIG NAME franchises can be bad. Here are a couple of examples:

1. An ice cream franchise inserted a clause into its contract that placed additional conditions on any franchise owner that wished to sell their business. This particular franchise required the existing owner to be the personal guarantor for the new owner. Essentially this meant that if the new owner did not live up to the contract provisions, the previous owner would become liable. In my mind, this is a "heads they win, tails you lose" situation. At one time, this franchise was so "hot" that they had multiple people wanting to buy most every territory. If one person did not agree to the contract, then the franchise company would move on to the next candidate. Many people ignored their attorney's advice (or didn't use an attorney) and signed on the dotted line. Their emotional perception of making a lot of money (i.e., "This is a goldmine, why would I ever want to sell?") got in the way of their logical side. This opportunity did not turn out well for many of the franchise owners.

2. A donut franchise included a clause in its contract that permitted the franchise company to require the owner to purchase new equipment if the location had been open for more than four years. When the franchise company's financials leveled off after a period of meteoric growth, the company's investors started to demand higher revenue and profit numbers. The easiest and fastest way for the company to increase their numbers was by requiring all eligible franchise owners to buy new equipment (approximately $700K to $1M). Since the company was selling the equipment directly to the owners there was a nice near-term bump to both revenue and profit. This required purchase of equipment came as a surprise to, and angered, many of the franchise owners.

They should have known better and anticipated the possibility because it was clearly stated in their contracts.

Never feel so caught up in the emotional wave that you can't walk away from a bad deal no matter how attractive it may seem at the time.

# Rule 12: Not All Great Franchises Are Great For You!

Why might a top franchise not be the right one for you?  It's all about 'fit.'  Think about it this way, a Lamborghini is a great car, especially if it's just you and your significant other driving on an empty highway (with no police around).  But, if this is your only car and its main purpose is to shuttle your 4 kids to the mall, soccer practice, etc., it's probably not the right car for you.

Take all of those "top franchise" ratings you'll find in "Inc.," "Entrepreneur," and other publications and throw them away (at least put them aside).  I'm never sure exactly what criteria their rankings are based on and with the information provided you wouldn't have any idea if you would be a great 'fit.'

Here's a good example: I worked with a man several years ago that had, before speaking to me, spent about 18 months going through the 'best of..." franchise lists, finding opportunities that looked interesting, and then investigating them one or two at a time.  One day he phoned me, explained his situation, stating that he was about to sign an agreement with one of the franchises he uncovered.  He really wasn't happy with type of "sales" required to make the business successful, but he was willing to move forward because he thought that he would be happier with the franchise than at the job he was looking to leave.  He wanted to perform one last search before committing himself, but said that he did not hold out much hope of finding a better 'fit' because he had already done all of this "best of..." pre-investigative work.

Following my process he learned that the opportunity he was close to buying wasn't a good 'fit' and within a few months found the great 'fitting' franchise that he had hoped for. Speaking to him nearly one year later, he told me that he had never seen his franchise on any of the "best of" or "top" lists, and was very thankful that we spoke before he pulled the trigger on his initial selection. He enjoys the day-to-day of running his business, and according to the friends and relatives that he has referred to me, is far happier than he ever was in corporate life.

There is often a big difference between a franchise that is a great 'fit' and the "best of" lists. Your goal should be finding a franchise where the most successful owners are people that are very similar to you (e.g., personality, attributes, goals, etc.). When you find a franchise like this, your chance of success greatly increases because the system is essentially built for people like you to be successful.

Of course, the opposite are franchises where you're most like the people who struggle. No matter how much you like the product or service the business offers, my advice would be to move on to another opportunity. If you're most like the franchise owners who struggle, aren't you going into your business with a severe disadvantage?

There are NO franchise concepts where everyone is successful. Remember the graphic from the last rule (20% of franchises are great, 60% good, and 20% bad)?

We can use a re-labeled version of that same graphic to demonstrate the success levels of the owners who operate one of those "great" franchises.

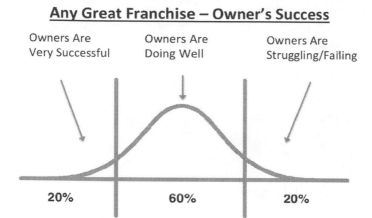

**Any Great Franchise – Owner's Success**

Owners Are Very Successful     Owners Are Doing Well     Owners Are Struggling/Failing

20%          60%          20%

What are the differences among the owners of even the most successful franchises?

1. The very successful owners will be a great 'fit' for the system. They likely did a great deal of due diligence before selecting the franchise. They spoke with many of the then-current owners (the successful and the struggling) and found that the most successful were very much like them.

2. The 60% in the middle are doing well. They're happy, yet know that they have room for improvement. When asked, the majority would likely make the same decision to buy the franchise all over again. They are a good 'fit' for the franchise system, but have areas in which they are not as proficient as the top 20%.

3. The 20% at the bottom will be afflicted with at least one of the following issues:

a. They don't follow the system! Why people buy a franchise and then ignore the proven systems for which they have just paid is a mystery to all of us in the franchise industry.

b. They are a bad 'fit!' If the business is in an industry that they love, some people will convince themselves prior to buying that they are a great 'fit.' What many people don't realize is that a great 'fit' is about the capabilities of the owner, not solely the love of the end product or service.

c. They blame everyone but themselves for the bad things that happen!

d. They didn't take the time to understand themselves (e.g., goals, skills, etc.) and their desired destination.

# Rule 13: Typewriters and Floppy Discs.

Periodically a client will tell me that he/she will only buy a franchise if there is a very high barrier to entry and/or no competition. I'll tell him/her (with a straight face) that I know a business broker who has typewriter and floppy disc businesses for sale if he/she truly wants no competition.

When you buy a franchise, rarely, if ever, will you be in a market without competition. Franchise companies look for well-established markets that have a lot of competition, with no one business having a significant market share (i.e., small independent businesses or mom-and-pops). The goal of a franchise is to quickly create a dominant presence in the market, and using their systems, build a market share that is disproportionate to the competition.

Let me provide a couple of examples:

1. In the early 1950s there were independent hamburger joints and lunch counters on almost every corner; franchise fast food wasn't a known entity at that time. Fast forward 50 or 60 years, greater than 90% of fast and casual dining has been consolidated into franchises.

2. Another example is men's haircutting. As of the 1960s and '70s most of (if not all) the barbershops were owner-operator businesses. Since then, the men's haircutting industry has become increasingly dominated by franchised brands; approximately 25% are franchises with their market share growing 1% to 2% per year.

There are many more examples like the two above. It's important to remember that competition is good; it indicates that there is a need for the product or service. The franchise (company and owner) makes money by providing a more efficient, consistent, convenient, and/or better offering to their customers than the independents.

# Rule 14: That Won't Work Here!

On occasion I have heard comments along the lines of, "I don't think that concept will work in New England because we have a great sense of self-reliance."[5]

There is little if any validity to these types of regional statements. Great and good franchise companies do not want to enter a region if the concept is a probable failure (imagine a franchise that sells spring water ice to Eskimos). If the concept does not work in a geographic area due to certain conditions (e.g., culture, laws, demographics, etc.), the franchise is likely to stay out. If you were to inquire about operating a location in one of these areas, the franchise would tell you that they are not selling territories in your market at that time.

Sometimes circumstances change. A franchise that has previously stayed out of your area may decide that the situation has become more attractive and is now looking for franchise owners. The franchise may have an established or popular brand in other parts of the country that you could capitalize on. It's like having a startup business backed by a successful brand name.

---

[5] I live and work in the greater Boston area, hence my New England reference. Similar versions of this statement are made all over the country.

# Rule 15: Once In A Lifetime Opportunities.

People have a tendency to let short-term enthusiasm (otherwise known as "get rich quick" dreams) get in the way of long-term judgment.[6] We think that we can't pass up an opportunity because it's a "once in a lifetime chance" and "we'll make so much money that we'll never want to sell." Stop before you violate **Rule 1**: **Don't Do Anything Stupid**. I've seen many instances of a franchise concept exploding into the market and the minds of the public (mostly in the food industry where brand names are most prominent). The franchise will seemingly appear from "nowhere" to being "everywhere" in a very short period of time.

Has there ever been such a thing as a "can't miss" business? One that everyone knew was going to be a big success, before it actually was.[7] How many products touted as such have actually worked out?  Also, if the business is in an industry that tends to be trendy/faddish, like ice cream,[8] think about the long-term.  How can you determine that the franchise you're thinking of acquiring will be one of the few to remain popular over a long period of time and not become just another brand in 2 or 3 years?

---

[6] The "get rich quick" premise is the basis of one of the greatest TV shows ever: *The Honeymooners*.

[7] Everyone is able to look back on an opportunity and say they knew that it was going to be a "big success." Funny thing is that almost no one who says that ever invests any money into the concept.

[8] Ice cream is not trendy/faddish, but ice cream franchises are.

Never believe that any franchise is such a "can't miss" opportunity that you must rush through your due diligence process, driven by the belief that someone else is about to buy "your" territory.  Take your time.  Speak with a sufficient number of existing franchise owners and hire a franchise attorney.  If you find yourself tempted to skip steps, think about the franchise owners in **Rule 11: Just Because It's A Franchise...** many of whom also skipped steps.

# Rule 16: Is It Negotiable?

This is a common question regarding the franchise contract. Let's get one major point out of the way first:

**ALL FRANCHISE CONTRACTS ARE HEAVILY WEIGHTED IN FAVOR OF THE FRANCHISE COMPANY!**

Don't be surprised or put off by this. Franchise companies have systems and intellectual property to protect, things that they will share with you when you become a franchise owner. Also, every franchise owner prior to you signed a similar contract. The franchise company is not taking advantage of or picking on you!

Even though heavily weighted in favor of the franchise company, there are some areas of the contract that can be negotiated (this is one of the many good reasons to hire a franchise attorney).

Areas that can't/won't be changed usually deal with monetary issues, such as franchise fees, royalty amounts/percentages, etc. Altering any of these items would require the franchise company to republish the FDD (Franchise Disclosure Document), which is a time consuming and expensive proposition. In addition, it can be very disruptive to the franchisee candidates who are in the process of investigating the opportunity.

For more on the importance of using a franchise attorney refer to **Rule 25: Use A Franchise Attorney Damn It...I Mean Please.**

# Rule 17: But The Franchise Person Said...

*"We never have and never plan to..."*

If a representative of the franchise ever makes a statement like this to you, don't believe it!

Any time you're dealing with a legal agreement you should always assume that...

**IF IT'S WRITTEN IN THE CONTRACT IT WILL BE ENFORCED!**

It does not matter what it is - a marketing fee that has never been collected, a performance clause that has never been enforced, or anything else. If it's in the contract, plan for it to happen no matter what the franchise company tells you, and build it into your business plan if it could impact your revenue and/or profit.

For clauses having to do with performance or quotas, the franchise company doesn't have to treat all franchise owners equally. If you're trying very hard, following the systems, and are a good team player, they may not enforce the clause. On the other hand, if you're a malcontent that causes the franchise more trouble than you're worth, they may decide to use the clause to usher you out of the system.

For marketing and/or advertising fees, the franchise company must be consistent. If they collect fees from one franchise owner, they must collect fees from all.

If you're concerned about a particular item in the contract (e.g., advertising fees) that the franchise claims they will never enforce ask them, "If you never plan to enforce/enact it, why not take it out of the contract or modify it?"[9] There are many possible responses to this question, so think about the answer you receive and factor it into your decision.

For example, one of my clients was investigating a consumer services franchise that required him to spend 10% of his revenue on marketing his business. He understood that the 10% was important in the early years to build his business. He was concerned that once he had maximized his territory it would not make economic sense to continue spending at the same rate. Under these conditions 10% would be a great deal of money that would yield essentially no additional market share (my client was willing to spend 2% or 3% per year after reaching the required sales goals to maintain market share). The franchise company was not able to provide a response other than they might consider changing the clause in the future. My client did not find this acceptable. After we had several discussions regarding the franchise company's position, I suggested he might want to consider similar franchises that did not have this requirement. After investigating one or two more concepts, he found a great 'fitting' franchise; one that had all of the positives of the original choice, but without the onerous marketing commitment.

---

[9] Modification/removal of a clause is possible if it does not require the FDD to be reissued.

# Rule 18: Franchises Are Safer But...

Entrepreneurial and business magazines regularly publish statistics that claim franchises are far safer than any other type of business. Like most statistics, the numbers can be massaged to look like anything the creator wants to convey. The figures that I see (or hear about) most often claim that franchises have a success rate of greater than 90%! My response is usually, "That's sounds great, but what criteria are they using to come up with that result?" For example, I've seen publications define success as a franchise location/territory that's been open for more than a certain number of years. That seems very positive, but they probably don't tell you how many owners that location had in that same period (one, two, or ten).

Don't take these success statistics at face value. You can't pick out any franchise and automatically have a greater than 90% chance of success. As a reminder revisit **Rule 12: Not All Great Franchises Are Great For You**.

Buying a franchise does not guarantee you any level of success! The better you 'fit' the franchise, the greater the chance of achieving your goals.

# Rule 19: My Neighbor's Cousin's Best Friend's Uncle.

There have been times I've spoken to a client about a franchise concept that I thought might be a great 'fit' for him/her. I'd even review his/her criteria (e.g., the "must have" and "like to have" attributes) when describing the concept so as to demonstrate the potential 'fit.' My client responded with something like, "My neighbor's cousin's best friend's uncle had a business similar to this in Nebraska and it failed, so I don't think I would be interested in looking at anything like this." I realize that this example is a bit far-fetched, but after hearing statements like this many times, that's what it sounds like to me.

After taking a deep breath, realizing that I have my work cut out for me, I ask him/her some of the following questions:

1. Have you ever met this person?

2. What exactly was the business that he owned?

3. Was it a franchise?

4. How did he find the business?

5. Was he a good 'fit' for the business?

...More questions as needed.

In most instances he/she hasn't the slightest idea of whom this person is or what he did/didn't do. My client had a preconceived notion of the business (and their chance of success) based upon a $3^{rd}$, $4^{th}$, or $5^{th}$ hand account.

It's very important to keep an open mind when presented with concepts.

There are only two reliable sources of franchise information that you should rely on to make a decision.

1. **The Franchise Company**: The franchise company must present you with the FDD (Franchise Disclosure Document) early in the education/sales process,[10] long before it's time to make a decision. The franchise will also take you through their systems at a high level. They will provide you with a lot of basic information, but it's like looking at a glossy brochure for a car. The information will be truthful and helpful, but you'll get much better information from those who actually operate one.

2. **The Franchise Owners:** The information gathered from existing owners will provide you with the best insight as to what it's like to be an owner. This step is vital to understanding if the opportunity will be a great 'fit' for you. Expect to learn about things like:

   a. Franchise company / franchise owner relations

   b. Company culture

   c. Effectiveness of initial training and ongoing support

---

[10] Some franchise companies won't provide you with thec FDD until you arrive at Discovery Day, during which they will review it with you. Although perfectly legal, I am not a fan of this process since it allows the franchise company to frame issues before you've had a chance to read and think about them.

d. Cost to open and operate the business

e. Revenue and profit potential

f. A typical day in the life of the owner

g. Would the owners buy this franchise again knowing then what they know now

Pre-investigation of a franchise opportunity, such as checking out the company website, grievance websites, or the input of friends/family is of little help. If the concept is something that seems to have potential, talk to the franchise company and franchise owners. Talking to the franchise company/owners and learning more does not mean that you're making a commitment to buy; you're just educating yourself.

# Rule 20: Inside Out?

A number of years ago I spoke with a couple that were contemplating career changes. They were both in the financial/investment sector and were very seriously considering franchises. They were interested in finding existing fast food restaurant locations that were struggling. Their objective was to buy them at a discount and turn them around. Both were very physically fit and extremely conscience about diet and nutrition.

Even though I didn't work with re-sale opportunities in the food industry, I assisted them as much as I could since a former client referred them to me. I helped the couple understand some of the basics of franchising and how to best investigate opportunities. During our initial discussions I mentioned that franchised restaurants are probably the most inflexible businesses in the industry. Margins on food products are very small and the market is very competitive. Fast food brands thrive by carving out niches in the market.

After several months of not hearing from them, they let me know that they had purchased a number of existing locations of a food concept that is not known for its healthy choices. This brand's niche was that they would serve you great tasting and very satisfying food, but if you had EVER asked about calories or nutritional content of a food item, you would not be a customer.

Being the curious type I asked about the apparent lack of 'fit' that existed between the couple's values and that of the food brand. They knew the concept did not 'fit' with their values, but were hopeful that once on the inside they could work to promote change to the culture and begin to integrate healthier choices into the menu.

This couple decided to sell their locations a year or two later due to the lack of 'fit' with the brand. They discovered that for most franchise owners, long-term success requires both a business and cultural 'fit.' The couple moved on to a different franchise opportunity, one that was a better all around 'fit.'

Never buy a franchise business thinking that you can affect changes to a long established, well-oiled franchise system. You'll be miserable, your business will suffer, and the franchise won't change. In the end you'll probably leave the franchise and sell your business at a loss.

# Chapter 3: Finding The Right Franchise

A Needle In A Haystack?

It Doesn't Have To Be!

# Rule 21: Use A Franchise Broker!

This rule should be a 100%, absolute, no brainer for you! Why?

1. Brokers should never charge you a fee for their services - it's FREE!! They operate like executive recruiters for franchise companies. If you select a franchise that the broker recommends, the franchise company pays the broker a commission. This commission has no bearing on what you pay for the franchise; the cost to you is EXACTLY THE SAME whether you found it on your own or used a broker (unless specified in the FDD).

2. The broker is doing the legwork for you. The best franchise 'fit' for you may not be one of the brands you see in the "top" or "best of" lists. How will you ever find out about other (or better) opportunities unless you utilize someone with industry knowledge? Refer to the example in **Rule 12: Not All Great Franchises Are Great For You!**

3. The broker should give you some type of test (at no cost) to assess your abilities/capabilities. This will help the broker narrow down the options, eliminating concepts that do not 'fit' your personality and skills.

4. A good broker should also take the time to understand your budget and income expectations. Make sure your broker understands how long you can live before you need to take money out of the business; remember that you need to budget for living expenses while growing your business to profitability.

5. A good broker should guide and assist you all the way through the franchise investigation process. If your broker disappears after he/she has recommended franchises to you, it may be time to find another broker.

For more about how to find and utilize a good franchise broker refer to:

**Chapter 4: Finding a Franchise Broker**

# Rule 22: It's Not Perfect.

A frequent reason people give for not buying a business, either now or in the past, is that they could not find the "perfect business."

There is no such thing as the perfect business, just as there is no such thing as the perfect spouse, job, house, etc.

You may have created a long list of "must-have" criteria for any business you'll consider. If there is no flexibility or compromise in your list, save your energy and admit that business ownership is not right for you. I have found that the quest for perfection is nothing more than an excuse that is used for not doing something.

If you had required perfection in any of the big steps you've taken in life (e.g., marriage, home purchase, kids, etc.), then you probably would've never moved out of your parents' house.

Rather than using your "must have criteria" as a way of giving a franchise business thumbs up or down, use it to evaluate the franchise against the alternative of a job. Which option has the ability to satisfy the most important items on your list?

# Rule 23: What or Why.

In my experience businesses are bought for one of two reasons. The first group buys because of the product or service the business provides (the WHAT). The second group buys because they believe that a business will help them accomplish their goals (the WHY). Is one better? Like most things in life, it depends.

Most people I work with buy a business because it helps them achieve the desired financial and lifestyle balance mentioned earlier (the WHY). If long-term goal achievement is your primary business ownership motivation, try to put aside WHAT the business does and focus on the WHY. I don't want you to take this suggestion to such an extreme that you would consider "any" business regardless of legal, moral, ethical, or personal considerations. It's OK to eliminate one or two concepts based upon your individual preferences, but don't make sweeping judgments as it may cause you to miss some great 'fitting' opportunities.

A very important point to remember is that in most cases you're running a business, not performing the function of the business. For example, successful CEOs are able to move among industries (e.g., autos, food, technology, etc.) regularly. They're not hired because they know about the products; [11] they know how to run a business and hire good people who know the products. In most cases the CEO doesn't even have a particular affinity toward the product.

---

[11] The CEO of Apple doesn't build IPhones. The CEO of BMW isn't on the assembly line. A maid franchise owner doesn't clean houses!

What the company does is, for the most part, secondary. They change companies because they see the opportunity as a better way to achieve their goals.

A smaller percentage of my clients buy a business based on the WHAT. They are far more interested in what the business is or does, and not so much on whether the business can help achieve their long-term goals. Most people who buy a WHAT business have already achieved many of their long-term goals, but still want to stay active in the business world. This is not a bad thing, but I would consider a venture like this to be more of a "hobby" business. There are a fair number of people who have opened wineries, golf shops, bed and breakfasts, or restaurants not because they were a great 'fit,' but because that's what they enjoy doing.

A somewhat similar rule focuses on logic versus emotion based buying. Looking logically at all of the aspects of a business will drive you toward buying a business based upon the WHY, whereas buying on emotion tends to be driven by the WHAT.

# Rule 24: Is "Sales" A Four-Letter Word?

No, it's actually five letters. The word "sales" comes with a great deal of negativity. We tend to think of salespeople as rude, obnoxious, pushy, and oblivious to our needs. When someone mentions "sales," common images are of people who sell used cars, life insurance, and time-share condos, etc. Many hate the thought of owning a business where they have to "sell," yet numerous everyday situations require us to convince others of something; in other words, "sell." Even convincing my wife to forego a chick-flick in favor of an action movie requires a form of selling.[12] Let's remove the negative connotation by thinking of "sales" as "customer/client acquisition," which we'll refer to as "acquisition."

In general, there are 3 types of "acquisition" roles for a business: Passive, Passive & Active, and Active. These designations overlap in many businesses, but for the purposes of this rule we'll assume they are distinct.

To make it easier let's refer to this graphic:

---

[12] Would you believe that she was the one who suggested I use this example?

**Customer/Client Acquisition Effort**

| 1 | 5 | 10 |
|---|---|---|
| Passive | Passive & Active | Active |

Starting with the least demanding of the roles, we'll work our way toward the most demanding:

1. Passive: Acquisition is accomplished by advertising (e.g., TV, Radio, Coupons, Direct Mail, Big Bright Neon Signs, etc.). Customers either call you to inquire about your service or they come into your store usually knowing what they want to buy; very little acquisition effort is required. Types of businesses that fall into this category include fast/casual food and many of the consumer services businesses (e.g., maids, house painting, lawn treatment/landscaping, dry cleaning, etc.).

2. Passive and Active: Acquisition occurs both directly and indirectly through networking in a variety of community and/or business organizations. While networking you may locate customers who need your product/service, but in the long run the majority of your business will come from networking generated referrals. These businesses are about relationship building. For example, damage mitigation businesses fall into the Passive and Active category. Let's say that the hoses of your washing machine fail resulting in severe flooding of your house. If the damage mitigation business were to receive a call directly from you, that would be Passive acquisition (you

likely found them via an online search). If they were to receive a call from your insurance agent, that would be Active acquisition (the owner acquired your business through networking and relationship building with the agent).

3. Active: Acquisition is very proactive and it's vitally important to always be prospecting for new clients. Most of these are Business-to-Business opportunities (e.g., language translation, sales force training, business coaching/mentoring, etc.). These are owner-centric businesses; the brand name has very little influence on the buyer. Success is dependent on you and the quality of the results.

NEVER overestimate your "acquisition" ability and desire. Here are two examples of past clients:

1. The first was an experienced saleswoman who spent twenty years in a high-pressure environment. She was very successful, but was tired of high-pressure sales and wanted to be in a business that required a less strenuous acquisition effort. At the same time, she didn't want something that was so removed that she couldn't develop relationships with her clients. She had a very high level of sales ability, but a lower level of desire, so she 'fit' very well into a business that required both Passive and Active acquisition. She bought, and is thriving at, a business in the education sector.

2. The second client was a former IT worker who had spent the past 12 years essentially locked in a computer room all day doing various tasks. When asked about his client acquisition ability and desire he responded, "I'll do anything I need to in order to be successful, even if it means making cold calls." His ability was low, but his desire was high. So what type of business was the best fit? A Passive acquisition business would be his best chance at success. Why? He said he would "do anything it took to be successful," and he may have for a while. But, I told him that in all probability he would quickly tire of the Active acquisition actions that success in this type of business requires. At that point he would begin procrastinating vital activities and/or giving off a negative vibe around potential clients. This would, in most cases, be the beginning of the end of his business.

Be honest with yourself! Determine which area (ability or desire) is your weakest, and then select a business in which the acquisition effort needed for success is a match.

# Rule 25: Use A Franchise Attorney Damn It... I Mean Please.

When you buy a franchise, you're entering into a legal contract with the franchise company in which each party has rights and responsibilities. Since you're also spending a significant amount of money (let's say somewhere between $50K and $500K) to purchase and open your business, don't try to save a little time and money (probably $2K or $3K) by not hiring an attorney to review the agreement. If a franchise company ever suggests that you could/should skip the attorney (e.g., "the contract is so simple, why waste your money?"), be cautious!

Once you've made the wise choice to use an attorney, you'll need to find one that understands franchising. Every area of legal expertise has its own subtleties and nuances. A lawyer that does not spend a significant amount of his/her time doing franchise work probably knows next to nothing about franchise law. If you were having issues with your heart, would you go to a cardiologist or a podiatrist? They're both doctors.

Here are a few reasons why you want a franchise attorney:

1. Based upon my clients' experience, your cost for a franchise attorney will probably be significantly cheaper (yes, I said cheaper) than a general business attorney. Franchise Disclosure Documents are long and boring,[13]

---

[13] You should always read the FDDs yourself and develop a list of questions about items you don't understand.

but much of what's in the document is legal boilerplate.[14] A franchise attorney should already be familiar with standard boilerplate language in the franchise agreement, and thus, will not have to spend as much time, or your money, parsing every word.

2. An attorney that does not specialize in franchises may be unfamiliar with some of the common red flags or anomalies in a franchise contract. This unfamiliarity could come back to cause you significant problems years down the road (see the two examples in **Rule 11: Just Because It's A Franchise**).

3. I've found that attorneys who don't understand franchise law can ruin a perfectly good deal. After dissecting the FDD, an attorney with little franchise experience will likely create a long list of contractual changes you should ask the franchise to make, which won't happen (see **Rule 16: Is It Negotiable?**). In most cases, the franchise company will be unhappy with your attorney's comments, and you'll be frustrated because you may feel that you're stuck between two immovable objects. At that point the franchise company may decide that the negatives of dealing with your attorney's lack of franchise knowledge outweighs the positives of having you join the team. In the end, only your attorney will be happy because he/she has learned franchise law on your dime.

---

[14] Boilerplate is important, but it's basically the same in every FDD.

The bottom line? Better safe than sorry. The franchise attorney might find nothing significant (or be able to affect some minor modifications) and you'll sleep better at night knowing that you won't be surprised by a contract clause in the future.

On the other hand, if the franchise attorney does find serious issues that the franchise company won't (or can't) change, you may want to think about passing on the opportunity and start looking for something else. A little money up front can save you a lot in the future.

A franchise attorney should never tell you to buy, or not buy, a specific concept. He/she will provide you with an understanding of what you're getting into before signing the contract. But, by the nature of your attorney's feedback (written and verbal), it should be fairly easy to discern his/her thoughts about the franchise.

How do you find a franchise attorney?

Finding a good franchise attorney is easy if you take these steps:

1. Ask your broker to recommend 2 or 3 franchise attorneys in the area. It's in the best interest of the broker to refer you to a knowledgeable franchise attorney, rather than one of those well-intentioned attorneys who doesn't have significant franchise experience.

2. During due diligence calls with other franchise owners in the area, ask if they can recommend a franchise attorney.

Before hiring the franchise attorney, ask them a few questions, such as:

1. What percent of their business is focused on franchises?

2. How many FDDs have they reviewed in the past year and for what franchises?

3. How many deals did their clients complete in the past year?

Look for an attorney who has significant franchise experience. He/she should have reviewed (or written) FDDs in multiple industries and have clients that have successfully completed deals with franchise companies.

# Chapter 4: Using Franchise Brokers

## I'm A Broker Now, But I Really Want To Direct.

# Rule 26: Who's My Broker?

What qualifies any broker to work with and help you find the right franchise?

Before you start working with a broker, ask him/her some questions:

1. How long has he/she been a franchise broker?

2. What else has he/she done in their career?

3. Has he/she owned a franchised business? (Other than their broker business that may also be a franchise.)

4. If he/she has owned a franchise, what was it and what happened to it?

I'm sure there are others that you will think of; the above is just meant to get you started. Like any excellent business relationship you'll want to have a strong rapport with your broker, after all you're depending upon him/her to provide you with a great deal of help and guidance.

**Suggestion**: Check out the broker's LinkedIn profile, as it will likely provide some excellent information on his/her background.

# Rule 27: You're Located Where?

Imagine that the latest addition to your family means that your current house is now too small and no longer fits your needs. You want to find a larger home that resides in a new neighborhood. To find the best new home, do you think that a real estate agent living in another state could provide you with the same level of expertise as an agent who lives locally? Most people I know would want to work with the local agent, a person who knows the school systems and the makeup of the community, and who has established an excellent reputation in the area.

Why should looking for a franchise business be any different? If the broker you're working with is local, he/she is going to know a lot more about the business environment (e.g., costs, competition, communities, etc.) than the broker who may be hundreds or thousands of miles away.

# Rule 28: Why Did You Recommend These Franchises?

Your broker should take you through some type of assessment test (at no charge to you) and have several discussions with you prior to recommending a few franchises to investigate. It's very important that you ensure the broker understands your goals and most important criteria!

As I am discussing franchise opportunities with my clients, I make sure to point out the 'fit' between their skills and those of the "top performers" in that franchise. I do this so that my clients understand why I'm suggesting particular opportunities. If the broker doesn't provide you with this insight, ask him/her.

Here are a few more potential questions for the broker:

1. How many times in the past 6 or 12 months has one of their clients purchased this franchise or one in the same industry?

2. Does the franchise broker's company/organization have a financial stake in any of the opportunities that they are suggesting?

There may or may not be any issues with these two areas, but it's good information to know.

# Rule 29: If You're Not Paying Them, Can You Trust Them?

I am periodically asked, "If you're paid by the franchise company, won't you show me the most expensive franchises so that you'll make the most money?"

There is essentially no correlation between the total cost to open your business and the broker's commission. Typically the broker is paid out of the franchise fee, which falls into a fairly narrow range for most franchises. For example, your cost to open a very popular fast food franchise may be about $2M, whereas a very popular residential/commercial painting franchise may cost you about $125K. What may amaze you is that the franchise fee you will pay in either case will be about $40K. The great difference in cost between the two opportunities is the food franchise's requirement that you build out a location to certain specifications and purchase certain equipment; these items have nothing to do with the broker.

Reminder: As noted earlier, your cost to buy and open a franchised business is exactly the same whether you use a broker or not.[15] If you use a broker, his/her commission will likely come from the franchise fee. If you don't use a broker, the franchise fee will be used for other marketing and franchise owner acquisition activities. Sorry, you don't get a discount for not using a broker (see footnote 15).

---

[15] Unless noted in the Franchise Disclosure Document.

As noted in earlier in **Rule 27: You're Located Where?**, I believe that it's important for your franchise broker to be local. The closer the broker, the more his/her reputation is based upon local clients and referral sources. As a franchise broker on the local level, my reputation is on the line each and every time I work with a client. Trying to convince a client to buy a business when they should get a job or buy the wrong business just because it pays a higher commission will quickly ruin my reputation.

# Rule 30: Are Franchise Brokers In The Yellow Pages?

Ask your kids this question and they may respond, "What are the Yellow Pages?"[16]

There are many ways of finding a great franchise broker, but the phone book is not one of them. Here are some recommendations:

1. Ask friends/colleagues who may have looked into franchising in the past if they can recommend a broker.

2. Contact a local SCORE[17] chapter (www.score.org) and ask if they can recommend someone in the area.

3. Contact a local Small Business Development Center (SBDC: www.asbdc-us.org) and ask if they have recommendations.[18]

4. If you're in a career transition group, ask if the coordinators or any of the members know a good broker.

---

[16] Or they may respond with the more kid-centric monosyllabic response of "Huh"?

[17] SCORE stands for the Service Corps of Retired Executives. They are a nonprofit association, with more than 300 chapters in the US, dedicated to helping small businesses get started, grow, and achieve their goals through education and mentorship.

[18] Both SCORE and SBDC are part of the US Gov't Small Business Administration (SBA).

On a side note, some brokers will "harvest" resumes off LinkedIn (as well as job search sites) and cold call/e-mail inquiring if you've ever considered business ownership. There is nothing wrong with a little initiative from brokers, but they must have a lot of free time on their hands to be making cold calls. I'm not a fan of this client recruiting method, but it's your decision.

# Chapter 5: Your Actions

You Get Out What You Put In.

# Rule 31: It's A Two Way Street.

As you begin to explore franchises, remember that the investigation and approval process is mutual. Just because you have the money doesn't mean that a good, let alone great, franchise will accept you. The franchise must believe that you will be a 'fit' for their system and culture. As you move through the process, always try to present your "best" to the franchise (see the next rule for examples). It's always better if you're offered the chance to join a franchise and turn them down, then want to join a franchise only to have them turn you down.

The same mutual relationship exists between you and the franchise broker. Even though you're not paying the broker, it's in your best interest to treat him/her with the same level of respect that he/she treats you.[19] After all, you're relying on him/her to help you determine the best path forward. It is not uncommon for a broker to "fire" a client who doesn't take the process seriously. The broker is making a decision to work with you just as you're making a decision to work with the broker. If your actions or inactions make the broker spend time trying to chase you down or get you to fulfill the commitments you've made, it's easier for the broker to move on to someone else.

---

[19] Although there is nothing preventing you from doing so, please only work with one broker at a time. If your current broker is not effective end the relationship and move on.

# Rule 32: Do You Treat Your Mother Like This?

Follow these steps and you'll look like a great candidate to the franchise and broker. Most of this is just about being considerate, which is easy for about 95% of you. This rule applies to the other 5%.

1. Return calls and e-mails from the franchise company and broker promptly.

2. Please don't drop a concept from consideration before the first call (or directly thereafter) with the franchise company. Once you tell the broker that you're interested in exploring a concept, commit yourself to at least 2 or 3 in-depth calls with the franchise representative. After several in-depth calls, you'll have a much better idea if the franchise might be a good 'fit.' If you "blow-off" the franchise before you complete a few calls, there's a chance you'll alienate your broker.

3. When you tell the franchise or broker that you're going to do something, do it. If you can't get to it by the expected date, let them know ahead of time.

4. If you can't keep a phone or in-person appointment, let the other person know at least one day ahead of time (emergencies excepted, of course) and always suggest some alternate days/times.

5. Ask the franchise representative questions! This shows interest and enthusiasm. If you're unsure as to what questions are appropriate, ask your broker if he/she can provide you with a list of general questions.

6. Don't suddenly drop off the face of the earth when working with a broker and/or franchise. Whenever this occurs I say that the person has gone "turtle." Picture someone hiding in his/her shell (avoiding all e-mails and phone calls) with the hope that the broker/franchise representative will tire and go away. There is no need to hide; "it's not right for me" is always an excellent answer. Don't worry about hurting our feelings; this is what we do for a living. By letting us know, you haven't burned any bridges and can always reengage if you change your mind. If you don't want to risk telling us "live" on the phone, send an e-mail at 3 a.m. It is appreciated.

# Rule 33: What Do You Discover At "Discovery Day?"

Discovery Day[20] provides you with the opportunity to travel to the franchise's headquarters location to meet with their executives and staff before you make a final decision. Since they have invited you, it's probable that they've already decided that you would be a good addition to the franchise (this assumes that you don't do anything to change their mind during your visit.[21]

Some franchises use the occasion to impart additional information about their concept. But, for the most part it's an upbeat event that's meant to get you excited about joining.[22]

Going to a Discovery Day is one of your final steps toward owning a franchise. Don't "jump the gun" by making the trip too early in your investigation, regardless of being invited by the franchise. Once you return most franchise companies will look for you to make a decision within 7 to 10 days and, if you haven't completed your basic due diligence, the chance of making a poor decision greatly increases.

---

[20] May also be known as a "Meet the Team" function.
[21] I have witnessed candidates get rejected solely based on their behavior at Discovery Day.
[22] The activities are likely to include other franchise candidates as well as some of the franchise HQ staff.

To insure that you get the most out of the Discovery Day experience, I suggest that you complete these tasks BEFORE you go!

1. Have your calls to other franchise owners completed.
2. Interview and select a franchise attorney (do not hire the attorney until you return and determine that you want to move forward).
3. Confirm that the franchise is a business 'fit' (i.e., that it can meet your long-term goals).
4. Have your financing plan well underway with a targeted completion date (if required).
5. Confirm that your significant other is on-board.
6. Ask the franchise company about their expectations and tell them about yours for Discovery Day and the days thereafter.

# Rule 34: Um... Pardon Me.

This will seem really obvious, but you might be surprised that on occasion a client will contact me with the following issue: the franchise representative promised to e-mail or call them with some information, but didn't. This is easily fixed. Politely contact the franchise representative and let them know you're waiting; franchise representatives are busy and once in a while some things fall through the cracks. You're not being pushy or insulting by reminding them and it shows a continued interest in the concept. If you're not able to get the information, ask your broker to contact the franchise representative as well.

## Rule 35: The First Impression.

All businesses have an "energy." As you go through each step in the investigative process (e.g., educational phone calls, franchise owner phone calls, Discovery Day, etc.) note how you're feeling. Do you feel excited (up) or are you worn out (demoralized). Much of that feeling can carry over into your business. To maximize your chance for success, you want a business that will energize you on almost a daily basis.[23]

In the early stages of investigation, issues (if any) will surround your relationship with the franchise's sales people. Franchise sales people tend to be very busy and are going through the same information with different prospects, hour after hour. Regardless, do they seem engaged or distant and disinterested? Are they cutting your scheduled time short? Are they late for calls? Can they answer your questions and, if not, do they get back to you with the answers without having to be reminded? If these situations are happening, are they one-time occurrences or do they happen regularly (assuming you've had more than one discussion)?

---

[23] This energy/excitement should come from your daily interactions with customers and employees, as well as any interactions you have with the headquarters staff.

These sales people are your first look at how the franchise company does business. Are you impressed or underwhelmed by them? Are they a reflection of the franchise culture or just an anomaly? You won't have much interaction with the sales people after you've purchased your franchise, but try to find out (e.g., calls with franchise owners, Discovery Day, etc.) if they're a reflection of the franchise company's attitude towards their franchise owners.

Don't sell short this part of the investigative process. It's very important that your franchise is not only a good business 'fit,' but a good cultural 'fit' as well.

# Rule 36: Business Partners.

Are you thinking about having a business partner (other than your spouse) who will be involved in buying and/or operating your franchise? A business partner could be an investor, working partner, etc.

Before bringing on a partner, you'll want an attorney to draw up a "partnership agreement" that covers all of the "what if" scenarios of life.

You and your partner may have been best friends for more than 30 years (all the way back to 5th grade) and always wanted to work together in a business. That's great, but what happens to the business if:

- One of you dies or becomes incapacitated?
- You end up not being best friends sometime in the future? Business relationships are different than personal relationships.
- One partner wants to sell his/her share?
- One of you turns into a slacker leaving the other with all of the work?

These and many other situations will be covered in the agreement. Get one! Your franchise attorney should be able to refer you to a business attorney if he/she cannot handle the task.

# Chapter 6: Final Thoughts

## I Did It My Way!

## Rule 37: It's Not Mardi Gras, But You Can Still Have Fun!

As you're going through the process of investigating franchise ownership, have fun. This is an educational experience and, at the end, you'll find that a franchise will be a great 'fit' for you or not. Either way, you're learning a lot about franchising and, more importantly, you're learning a lot about yourself.

Also remember that all you're spending during the vast majority of this process is your time. Your first outlay of money will probably not be until you (and hopefully your significant other, if you have one) attend a Discovery Day. That step is far down the road from where you are right now.

# Rule 38: It's Your Decision!

When you get to the point of making a decision (to buy or not buy a franchise) there will ALWAYS be a leap of faith involved. If the leap looks relatively small (such as over a water filled gutter on the street), then you're probably feeling confident that this is the right move. On the other hand, if the leap looks like the Grand Canyon (another gutter filled with water, but on a completely different scale), then something isn't right; don't be afraid to let the broker and/or franchise representative know. In some cases you may be experiencing last minute anxiety (see **Rule 9: Boo!**), while in others it may be that the business is not the right 'fit.' Review your initial reasons for buying a franchise and determine if anything has changed or if the opportunity is not a good match.

The entire process of achieving your goals starts with finding a franchise that's a great 'fit,' following the systems, asking for help when you need it, being a great team member, and not blaming others.

Every decision you make during this process is yours. For every correct decision, take pride. For every mistake, learn from it and try not to do it again.

## In Closing.

If you buy a franchise, your level of success will be because of you. At the same time, remember that you're not stranded on an island without access to help. The good and great franchises should be there to provide additional support, training, guidance, and expertise if you ever need it. This resource should not only be available during your early months, but for as long as you're a franchise owner. Never be too proud to ask for or accept help from the franchise company or other franchise owners. Franchising is a situation where "you're on your own, but never alone!"

I hope that these rules help you determine if a franchise is the best way to achieve your goals.

# About The Author

Mike has been involved in franchising for more than a decade. He is currently the owner of FranNet New England (part of FranNet LLC, the oldest and most trusted name in franchise brokering). Previously, he was a Master Franchise owner for ActionCoach.

Mike's other business activities include:

- President and Board of Directors: Heirloom Coffee, LLC
- Treasurer and Board of Directors: Association of Career Professionals - New England
- Founder: TestFile (a.k.a FratFile), an Internet Information Content Business
- Executive Positions at Various Small and Large Technology Corporations

Mike currently lives in the Boston, Massachusetts area with his family.

You may e-mail Mike at: Mike@TheFranchiseRULES.com.

Made in the USA
Charleston, SC
19 August 2014